Grayslake Area Public Library District
Grayslake, Illinois

1. A fine will be charged on each book which is not returned when it is due.

2. All injuries to books beyond reasonable wear and all losses shall be made good to the satisfaction of the Librarian.

3. Each borrower is held responsible for all books drawn on his card and for all fines accruing on the same.

THE BLACK POWER
MOVEMENT

by Rebecca Rissman

Content Consultant
Ibram X. Kendi, PhD
Assistant Professor, Africana Studies Department
University at Albany, SUNY

Core Library

An Imprint of Abdo Publishing
www.abdopublishing.com

Published by Abdo Publishing, a division of ABDO, PO Box 398166, Minneapolis, Minnesota 55439. Copyright © 2015 by Abdo Consulting Group, Inc. International copyrights reserved in all countries. No part of this book may be reproduced in any form without written permission from the publisher. Core Library™ is a trademark and logo of Abdo Publishing.

Printed in the United States of America,
North Mankato, Minnesota
022014
092014

Editor: Holly Saari
Series Designer: Becky Daum

Library of Congress Cataloging-in-Publication Data
Rissman, Rebecca.
  The Black Power movement / by Rebecca Rissman ; content consultant, Ibram H. Rogers, PhD, Assistant Professor, Africana Studies Department, University at Albany, SUNY.
    pages cm. -- (African-American history)
  ISBN 978-1-62403-144-1
1. Black power--United States--Juvenile literature. 2. Black Panther Party--Juvenile literature. 3. African Americans--Civil rights--History--20th century--Juvenile literature. 4. Civil rights movements--United States--History--20th century--Juvenile literature. I. Title.
  E185.615.R5217 2015
  323.1196'07309046--dc23
                    2014000104

Photo Credits: Bettmann/Corbis/AP Images, cover, 1; AP Images, 4, 12, 14, 17, 20, 26, 32, 45; Red Line Editorial, 7, 29; Dick DeMarsico/Library of Congress, 8; Herman Hiller/Library of Congress, 10; Bettmann/Corbis, 19; LB/AP Images, 23; JLP/AP Images, 31; David F. Smith/AP Images, 34; Sal Veder/AP Imagess, 37; John Rooney/AP Images, 39

CONTENTS

Y
323.1194
R15
12.14

CHAPTER ONE

AFTER THE CIVIL RIGHTS MOVEMENT

The civil rights movement in the United States occurred between 1954 and 1965. It was a time when people fought hard to earn rights for African Americans. The movement led to the Civil Rights Act of 1964 and the Voting Rights Act of 1965. Before then segregation and discrimination against African Americans was common in the South. The two acts made discrimination based on race against the

During the civil rights movement, people held protests and marches to demand civil rights for African Americans.

law. They also made segregation against the law. But equality for African Americans was still a long way off.

Poverty and Violence Remain

Even with the new laws, negative stereotypes about African Americans made it hard for them to get fair treatment from some whites. African-American schools had fewer resources than white schools. Landlords would rent to African Americans only in run-down neighborhoods. African Americans were often kept from good paying jobs. This meant many African Americans lived in poverty.

Violence against African Americans was also a problem, especially in the South. Whites often went unpunished if they committed crimes against African Americans. Lynchings of African Americans happened often. Lynchings occurred when a mob of people publicly hung a person. Sometimes African Americans were lynched without committing a crime. African Americans sometimes faced violence and harassment by police too.

Lynchings in the United States

This map shows where lynchings took place between 1882 and 1968. How does this information compare with what you read in the text? How can this map help you understand the text better?

A New Movement

The civil rights movement had focused on nonviolent resistance. Its goal was to convince Americans to believe in equality of all people. Martin Luther King Jr. was a leader in the movement. He believed in peaceful protests. He thought they were the best

Martin Luther King Jr. believed peaceful action was the best way for African Americans to gain equality.

way to get Americans to listen to the messages of the movement.

Some African Americans grew frustrated with this though. They wanted more from the movement.

African Americans were still being treated unfairly in the United States. Violence against African Americans was not taken seriously by law enforcement.

In 1965 the black power movement began. It wanted African Americans to gain more power in their communities. Members wanted to force Americans to accept equality. They also wanted to show the unfair treatment African Americans faced. Members of the black power movement held rallies and marches. They also gave speeches. The black power movement used strong and forceful language to make their message heard.

Malcolm X

Malcolm X was a famous African-American activist. He believed in the goals of the black power movement. Malcolm X was upset by the violent crimes committed against African Americans. He knew from history that changes in society often occurred with violence. Because of this he told African Americans they should achieve freedom and power "by any means

Malcolm X believed self-defense actions might be needed for African Americans to gain power.

necessary." This included violence. He told his followers they did not need a peaceful revolution.

Black Power Movement Grows

Martin Luther King Jr. disagreed. He thought peaceful protests were best. The differences between these two leaders showed the shift that was taking place in the United States. Many African Americans wanted more from the civil rights movement. They supported the forceful message of black power more than peaceful protests. In 1965 Malcolm X was shot and killed. His murder made him an icon in the black power movement. It helped the movement grow stronger.

Changing Nonviolent Message

The Student Nonviolent Coordinating Committee (SNCC) was founded in 1960. It started as a nonviolent civil rights organization for African-American and white activists. By 1965 SNCC changed its message of nonviolence. It also no longer preached the integration of races. It encouraged African Americans to do what was needed to gain political and economic power in their communities. This meant self-defense if necessary. SNCC also changed its membership rules that year. Now only African Americans could be members.

CHAPTER TWO

A TIME FOR ACTION

Stokely Carmichael became a well-known activist during the civil rights movement. By 1966 he was upset by how slowly change occurred for African Americans. Carmichael gave an angry speech after an African-American man was shot and killed. He said African Americans needed to take over their own communities. He said, "What we gonna start saying now is black power!"

Stokely Carmichael made the phrase *black power* popular.

As the message of black power spread, some people feared the movement might lead to African-American supremacy.

The Meaning of Black Power

For Carmichael the phrase *black power* was a call for African Americans to unite. It stood for working together to improve their communities. It meant taking pride in their culture. The most important message of black power was for African Americans to gain economic, political, and cultural control of their communities. They also needed to demand fair and equal treatment.

Against Black Power

Some people responded to black power with fear or distrust. The National Association for the Advancement of Colored People (NAACP) did not think people who supported civil rights and integration could support black power. The NAACP believed the black power movement was against these things. It thought the movement might lead to a feeling of African-American supremacy. This would be just as bad as white supremacy. Many white people feared black power was a war cry for violence against whites.

NAACP

The NAACP was founded in 1909. Its goal was to end discrimination and violence against African Americans. It wanted to make sure African Americans had the rights given to them in the US Constitution. Martin Luther King Jr. often worked with the NAACP. The NAACP believed in the nonviolent methods of the civil rights movement.

Black Panthers

In October 1966, Huey Newton and Bobby Seale founded the Black Panther Party for Self-Defense in Oakland, California. This group believed in socialism. This is system of governing that is controlled and led by the community rather than a set of individuals.

The Black Panthers liked socialism. It was a type of government that could work only if all people had equal rights and worked together.

The Black Panthers wanted equality and power in housing, education, and employment. They also wanted civil rights. The Black Panthers wanted to create true unity for

Kwanzaa Created

Maulana Karenga founded US Organization in 1965. In 1966 he created Kwanzaa. The holiday celebrates African heritage through song, dance, food, and togetherness. It lasts seven nights. Each night a candle is lit on the kinara, or candleholder. This stands for one of the seven ideals of Kwanzaa. They are unity, self-determination, working together, cooperative economics, purpose, creativity, and faith.

With the help of the Black Panthers, Huey Newton hoped African-American communities would gain power.

all people no matter their race, gender, or religion. The Black Panthers believed in the black power movement. They believed it could help African Americans overcome challenges. The Black Panthers became an important group in the black power movement.

Embracing African-American Culture

The history of slavery, discrimination, and racist writings led many people to believe African Americans

EXPLORE ONLINE

Chapter Two discusses some of the goals of the Black Panthers. The website below also focuses on their goals. As you know, every source is different. How is the information given in the website different from the information in this chapter? What information is the same? How do the two sources present information differently? What can you learn from this website?

Ten Points Program
www.mycorelibrary.com/black-power-movement

Those in the black power movement gathered together to demand equality and power in their neighborhoods.

were not equal to whites. The black power movement told African Americans to be proud of their heritage. One group that worked to spread African-American pride was US Organization. It became a major black power group. It encouraged members to wear their hair naturally. Members also wore traditional African clothing as a sign of pride. Colleges offered more courses in African-American history and literature. The black power movement was growing.

CHAPTER THREE

A TIME OF CHANGE

n 1967 the US Supreme Court ruled laws preventing people of different races from marrying were unconstitutional. This ruling brought attention to the unequal treatment of different races that still existed in the United States. It also reminded people that the government had a lot of work to do. Some people in the black power movement did not want to wait for the government to take action.

Although there had been some gains, African Americans were still protesting for equality in the late 1960s.

Black Arts Movement

The black arts movement occurred alongside the black power movement during the 1960s. It provided Americans with a huge burst of African-American literature, art, and music. African-American artists used the black power movement as inspiration for their work. These artists used their art to raise awareness of the challenges African Americans still faced. They wanted their art to encourage resistance.

Race Riots

In some communities, the Black Panthers patrolled the police. This was to keep African Americans safe from police violence. Tension was high between the two groups. Sometimes shootouts and skirmishes occurred with the police.

The tense environment between the black power movement and police sometimes led to race riots. In 1967 police pulled over cab driver John Smith for a minor traffic offense in Newark, New Jersey. The police arrested Smith, who was an African American. Then they beat him. News

A group of African-American men were stopped and searched by the National Guard during the Newark race riots.

of Smith's arrest and beating spread. A group of rioters quickly took to the streets to protest this unfair treatment. The riot lasted for six days. Twenty-three people died. More than 1,500 were arrested.

That same year, police officers raided a bar in an African-American neighborhood in Detroit, Michigan. The bar had broken a city rule. The African-American customers felt the police were kicking them out of the only place they felt comfortable. Soon their anger spread. A riot began. It lasted for five days.

Many buildings were destroyed or looted. Forty-three people were killed. More than 7,000 people were arrested.

The Vietnam War

While the black power movement was growing, the US military was fighting overseas in the Vietnam War. Many people felt African-American soldiers were treated unfairly during the war. Some people felt more African-American men than white men were being drafted into the war. Others felt African-American soldiers were given more dangerous assignments than white soldiers.

The black power movement considered the Vietnam War an example of the unfair treatment African Americans faced. Leaders in the movement criticized the US government for spending money on the war. They said it should have spent the money to improve poor African-American neighborhoods at home.

During the riots and racial violence of 1967, Martin Luther King Jr. gave a speech called "The Black Power Defined." In it he urged African Americans to work together:

> *We need organizations that are permeated with mutual trust, incorruptibility and militancy. Without this spirit we may have numbers but they will add up to zero. We need organizations that are responsible, efficient and alert. We lack experience because ours is a history of disorganization. But we will prevail because our need for progress is stronger than the ignorance forced upon us. If we realize how indispensable is responsible militant organization to our struggle, we will create it as we managed to create underground railroads, protest groups, self-help societies and the churches that have always been our refuge, our source of hope and our source of action.*

> Source: Martin Luther King Jr. "The Black Power Defined." TeachingAmerican History.org. *TeachingAmericanHistory.org*, n.d. Web. Accessed July 17, 2013.

What's the Big Idea?

Read this text closely. What is King saying to African Americans? What is his main point in the text? Choose two details from his speech that support this point.

CHAPTER FOUR

THE MOVEMENT WEAKENS

Black power leaders told African Americans to take strong actions to achieve change. Black Panthers raised their fists into the air to show they stood strong together. Sometimes violence occurred between police and black power members. But the majority of black power movement activities were nonviolent.

Riots broke out in Washington, DC, after Martin Luther King Jr. was assassinated.

Black Power at the Olympics

In 1968 two US Olympic medal winners brought black power to the world stage. African-American medal winners Tommie Smith and John Carlos stood on the awards podium. They raised their fists in the air as the National Anthem played. It was the black power salute. Many criticized this act. They felt it took attention away from the games. However, it also brought worldwide attention to the black power movement.

King Assassinated

On April 4, 1968, one of the strongest supporters of nonviolence was killed. Martin Luther King Jr. was assassinated by James Earl Ray, a white racist. People around the world were angry and upset after the assassination. Black power activists felt especially upset about King's death. It made their message seem even more important. King had been a symbol of peace and equality. They felt his murder showed whites still did not want to give African Americans equal rights. Riots broke out in more than 100 cities in the United States. When the riots ended,

Chicago Riot, 1968	
Deaths	11
Rioters wounded by police gunfire	48
Wounded policemen	90
Arrests	2,150
Buildings destroyed by fire	162
National Guard troops present	3,000

By the Numbers

After King's assassination, race riots broke out throughout the country. This chart shows how great an effect they had on just one city: Chicago, Illinois. How does the information shown compare to what you have learned from the text?

law enforcement and black power leaders still felt tension between them.

Fair Housing Act

One week after King's assassination, President Lyndon Johnson signed the Civil Rights Act of 1968. It is also known as the Fair Housing Act. This new law made it illegal to discriminate against race, gender, or religion

African-American Women

African-American women felt they were treated unfairly by US society during the black power movement. They also felt treated poorly by African-American culture and the black power movement. Women worked to raise awareness of the unequal treatment African-American women faced. They made many people think about how African-American women were treated. In 1974 a woman named Elaine Brown was appointed to lead the Black Panthers. This was a huge victory for African-American women.

in housing. This act was designed to help African Americans move into neighborhoods where only whites lived.

Those in the black power movement thought the act would help them gain power and equality in their neighborhoods. But the Fair Housing Act did not work well in practice. Some white people did not want to share their neighborhoods with African Americans. Many whites left cities and moved to the suburbs. African Americans again felt they were treated with prejudice.

The Fair Housing Act led to some integration of neighborhoods.

Different Ideas for Black Power

Groups within the black power movement sometimes disagreed about how to achieve their goals. But in the late 1960s, tension about this increased. The Black Panthers focused on socialism as a way to get black power. They wanted to form a new government

Groups of the black power movement were starting to break apart in the late 1960s.

that would be controlled by the working class. US Organization thought it was more important to focus on African culture and heritage. They believed

FURTHER EVIDENCE

In Chapter Four, you learned that King's murder was followed by riots, violence, and fear. Try to identify one of the chapter's main points. What evidence can you find that supports this point? Then go to the website below to read the lyrics of a song by the musical group Sly & The Family Stone. It was released just months after King's death. Does the information on this website support the main point in this chapter? Write a few sentences on how the information from the website helps you understand the chapter.

"Everyday People"
www.mycorelibrary.com/black-power-movement

African Americans would gain power by going back to their roots. The two groups became hostile toward one another. This weakened the black power movement.

CHAPTER FIVE

THE MOVEMENT'S END AND LEGACY

In 1956 the Federal Bureau of Investigation (FBI) started the Counter Intelligence Program (COINTELPRO). Its purpose was to weaken groups the FBI thought were too revolutionary. COINTELPRO focused on the black power movement soon after the movement started.

COINTELPRO wanted to prevent the black power movement from growing.

COINTELPRO's Effect

COINTELPRO worked to turn black power movement members and groups against each other. The program wanted the groups to destroy themselves. It fed false stories to the press that made black power groups look bad. It planted evidence that made Black Panthers members look like they were working against the group. This caused members within the group to turn on one another. In 1971 the Black Panthers split up. The Black Panthers had been the leading group of the black power movement. This split weakened the movement.

The Greatest Threat

John Edgar Hoover was the director of the FBI from 1924 to 1972. He called the Black Panthers "the greatest threat to the internal security of the United States." Hoover wanted the COINTELPRO program to decrease the group's power and stop the group and the black power movement from growing.

When the Black Panthers split, it negatively affected the black power movement.

Coming to an End

The focus of black power groups changed in the 1970s. In 1974 black power leaders met in Washington, DC, to discuss the future of the movement. Some groups wanted to focus on socialism. Others wanted to focus on strengthening African-American culture and communities. The groups could not agree on a path forward. The black power movement split even more. By 1975 the

Black Panther Assassinations?

Black Panther leaders Mark Clark and Fred Hampton were killed in a 1969 police raid in Chicago, Illinois. Law enforcement claimed that the Black Panthers took part in a shootout with the police. However, many officials in the black power movement claimed the two men had been murdered. A later investigation showed the Panthers had fired only one shot. Police had fired between 82 and 99. The officers were never punished for their actions. Some people have believed COINTELPRO arranged for the two Black Panther leaders to be assassinated.

movement came to an end.

The Legacy of Black Power

The black power movement came to a close when the different groups disagreed on how African Americans should move forward. Still the movement achieved great things. It raised awareness of the struggles faced by African Americans. More US citizens now knew about the police violence that African Americans sometimes faced.

The black power movement helped African Americans take back power politically, socially, and economically.

They knew about the injustices black power groups were fighting to end.

The movement helped African Americans gain power in their communities. It also helped African Americans embrace their heritage. The movement has inspired many activists. People use the ideals of the black power movement to fight for power and equality around the world.

In 1968 Bobby Seale gave a speech that discussed racism in the black power movement. He clarified that black power is not a movement against white people:

> *When the man walks up and says that we are anti-white I scratch my head. . . . I say . . . That's your game, that's the Ku Klux Klan's game. . . . I wouldn't murder a person or brutalize him because of the color of his skin. I say yeah, we hate something alright. We hate the oppression that we live in. . . . If you got enough energy to sit down and hate a white person just because of the color of his skin, you're wasting a lot of energy. You'd better take that same energy and put it in some motion out there and start dealing with those oppressive conditions.*

> Source: William L. Van DeBurg. New Day In Babylon: The Black Liberation Movement and American Culture, 1965–1975. *Chicago: University of Chicago Press, 1992.*
> *Print. 20.*

Consider Your Audience

Review this passage closely. Consider how you would change it for a different audience, such as your parents, your principal, or younger friends. Write a blog post giving this same information to the new audience. How does your new approach differ from the original text and why?

IMPORTANT DATES

1956

1964

1965

The Counter Intelligence Program (COINTELPRO) forms at the FBI. It later focuses on stopping the black power movement and the Black Panthers.

The Civil Rights Act of 1964 is signed into law. It makes racial discrimination in jobs and segregation illegal.

Malcolm X is assassinated on February 21.

1967

1968

1968

Race riots break out in New Jersey and Michigan, leaving 66 people dead.

Martin Luther King Jr. is assassinated on April 4, causing riots throughout the United States.

President Lyndon Johnson signs the Civil Rights Act of 1968. It makes discrimination in housing illegal.

1965

The Voting Rights Act passes. It makes discrimination at voting locations illegal.

1966

Stokely Carmichael introduces the term *black power*.

1966

Huey Newton and Bobby Seale form the Black Panthers.

1968

At the Olympics, John Carlos and Tommie Smith raise their fists in the black power salute.

1971

The Black Panthers split up.

1975

The black power movement comes to an end.

STOP AND THINK

You Are There

This book discussed some of the race riots that occurred during the black power movement. Imagine you are living in Detroit during the race riots of 1967. What do you think about the violence? Do you think the rioters are helping or hurting the black power movement? How would you explain the reason for the riots to a friend living in another city?

Tell the Tale

Chapter One explains how life after the civil rights movement was still difficult for African Americans. Imagine you are an African-American student living in the 1960s. Write a journal entry describing what a day is like for you and your family. What challenges do you face? Be sure to set the scene, develop a sequence of events, and offer a conclusion.

Say What?

Reading about African-American history can involve learning new vocabulary words. Write down five words in this book that you didn't know. Then look them up in the dictionary. Read the definitions and rewrite them in your own words on note cards. Ask a friend to quiz you on your new vocabulary words.

Surprise Me

Chapter Five discusses the COINTELPO program that worked against the black power movement. Did it surprise you to learn this happened? What did you find most surprising about it? Write a few sentences about each fact.

GLOSSARY

activist
a person who works to bring about political or social change

assassinate
to murder an important person for political, religious, or social reasons

discriminate
to treat someone unfairly based on differences, such as race or gender

heritage
the valued history and traditions of a culture or group of people

integrate
to bring people who were once segregated back into another group

oppress
to keep down by cruelty or injustice

prejudice
hatred or unfair treatment due to having fixed opinions about a group of people

raid
a sudden attack or search

riot
a large-scale, violent uprising of a crowd

segregate
to involuntarily separate or keep people apart from another group

unconstitutional
not in agreement with the constitution of a government

LEARN MORE

Books

Gormley, Beatrice. *Malcolm X: A Revolutionary Voice*. New York: Sterling, 2008.

Tarrant-Reid, Linda. *Discovering Black America: From the Age of Exploration to the Twenty-First Century*. New York: Abrams Books for Young Readers, 2012.

Websites

To learn more about African-American History, visit **booklinks.abdopublishing.com**. These links are routinely monitored and updated to provide the most current information available. Visit **www.mycorelibrary.com** for free additional tools for teachers and students.

INDEX

ABOUT THE AUTHOR

Rebecca Rissman is an award-winning author and editor of children's nonfiction. She has written more than 100 books about history, science, and art. She lives in Portland, Oregon, with her husband and enjoys hiking, yoga, and cooking.